The *Silver* Series of Puppet Plays

§ Edited by **Lisl Beer**§

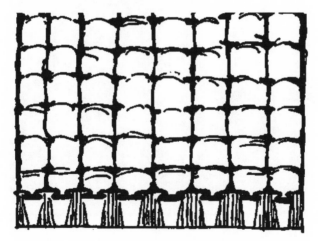

THE SECOND SHEPHERD'S PLAY

Adapted from the *Townley* Manuscript

By

Lisl Beer

Print Edition 9780828312462

BRANDEN BOOKS, Boston
www.brandenbooks.com

Print Edition ISBN 9780828312462

Branden Books PO Box 812094 Wellesley MA 02482
www.brandenbooks.com

THE SECOND SHEPHERD'S PLAY
CAST OF CHARACTERS
COLL - *First Shepherd*
GYB- *Second Shepherd*
DAW- *Third Shepherd*
MAK - *A Poor Fellow*
GILL - *His Wife*
THE ANGEL OP THE NATIVITY
THE VIRGIN MARY AND INFANT JESUS

SCENE I: *An Open Field*
                              COLL

Lord, but these weathers are cold, and I am ill-happed,
I am but nearly dazed, so long have I napped.
My legs, they fold, my fingers are chapped.
It is not as I would, for I am all lapped
        In sorrow.
In storms and tempest
Now in east, now in west,
Woe to him that has never rest,
        Mid-day nor morrow.

But we silly shepherds that walk on the moor,
In faith, we're near homeless out of the door.
No wonder, as it stands, that we be poor,
For the till of our lands lies fallow as the floor.
        As ye ken
We are so hammed,
Over-taxed and rammed,
We are made hand-tammed
        By these gentlemen.

There comes a swain proud as a po;
He borrows my wagon, my plough also,
And I must grant it, ere he go.
Thus live we in pain, in anger and woe,
　　By night and day.
He must have it, if he long for it.
If I should forego it
I better be hanged for it
　　Than say him nay.

It does me no good when I walk by my lone,
Of this world to talk, to grumble and moan.
To my sheep will I stalk, and hearken anone.
There abide on a log, or sit on a stone
　　Full soon.
For I trow, pardie,
True men, if any there be,
I shall have more company,
　　Ere noon.

(Enter GYBJ

GYB

Benedicite Dominus (He gives a mock blessing.) What does
　　this mean?
Why fares the world thus? This life we've oft seen, Lord,
'tis spiteful and grievous, this weather so keen,
And the frost is so sharp, it waters my e'en.
　　There's no lie!
Now in dry, now in wet,
Now in snow, now in sleet,
My shoes freeze to my feet
　　Till I die! *(Snow falls slowly.)* So

far as I ken, wherever I go,
We married men suffer mickle woe.
We have sorry again, it befalls oft so.
Silly Capel, our hen, runs to and fro.
    She cackles,
But if she begin to croak,
To grumble, to sluck,
Then woe be to our cock,
He's in the shackles!

For if ever I read epistle, I have a wife by my fire
As sharp as a thistle, as rough as a briar,
She has brows like a bristle, and a sour face by 'er.
Once she wets her whistle, she sings clearer and higher
    Her *Pater Noster.*
She's as big as a whale,
She has a gallon of gall,
By him that died for us all —
    I wish I had lost her!

COLL
God, hark at the row!   Like a deaf man ye stand.

GYB

Yea, sluggard, the devil burn thy maw with his brand.
Didst see aught of Daw?

COLL

                Yea, in the pastureland I heard him
blow horn.   He be near at hand
        Below there. Stand still!

GYB

Why?

COLL

                    Here he comes; hope I
He'll tell us both some lie
Unless we beware

(Enter DAW.;
               DAW

There was never since Noah's flood such weather seen.
Wind and rain, and storms so keen,
Some stammer, some stand in doubt, I ween.
God turn it all to good!   I say as I mean.
   Look yonder!
How these snows all drown
The fields and the town
And bear all down,
      'Tis a wonder!

Ah, Sirs, God save you, and my master sweet!
A drink I crave, and summat to eat!

COLL

Christ's curse, you knave, you're a lazy cheat!

GYB

Look how he rave, wait till later for meat!
   We have et it!

I'll thrift on thy pate! *(laughs)*
Though the rogue came late
He will dine in state
    To eat, if he could get it!

(COLL *and* GYB *are doubled up laughing.*)

DAW

Such servants as I, that sweat and swink,
at our bread full dry, I needs must think,
For late we come by our dinner and drink,
    But soon thereto
Our lady and our sire,
When we've been in the mire,
Take a cut from our hire,
    Pay as slow as they care to.

COLL

Thou'rt an ill lad to be grumbling,
For a man had but little for spending!

GYB

Peace, boy, I bid, no more wrangling.
I'll make thee full sad, by the King
    With thy gauds—
Where be our sheep, boy? Left alone?

DAW

Sir, this same day at morn
I left them in the corn

While they rang *Lauds.*
They have pasture good, they cannot go wrong.
That's right, by the Rood, these nights are long.
Ere we go now, 1 would someone gave us a song.

GYB

So I thought, as 1 stood, to beguile us along.

DAW

I agree.

COLL

The tenor I'll try.

GYB

I'll sing treble so high,

DAW

Then the lowest shall be I.
Come, chant, now, let's see!

(They sing an old song, "Holly and the Ivy.")
(Enter MAK *wrapped in a cloak over his smock.)*

MAK

Now, Lord, by thy seven names' spell
That made moon and stars, Heaven and Hell,
By thy will with me, more than I can tell,
　　　Lord, lack I.
I am at odds, naught goes well, it doth my temper try.

Would I might in heaven dwell, where no children cry,
So still . . .

COLL

Who's that, pipes so poor?

MAK

Would God ye knew what I endure!

COLL *(with sarcasm)*.

There's a man who walks on the moor
And has not all his will! *(All laugh.)*

GYB

Come, Mak, whither do you speed, what news do you bring?

DAW *(pretending surprise}*

Is Mak come? Then take heed everyone to his thing!
(Playfully snatches at MAK's *cloak.)*

MAK

Let be! I'm a yeoman of the king
And a messenger from a great lordling
And . . , *(any name)* the like thereby.
Fie on you, get hence
Out of my presence!
I must have reverence!
    Dare you ask, who am I?

COLL

Why dress ye so cute, Mak, ye do ill.

GYB

Listen, ye saint, I believe what ye will!
(Laughs broadly.)

DAW

How the knave can joke, the devil him kill!

MAK *(nastily).*

I'll make a complaint, and ye'll all get your fill
    At a word from me!
I'll tell your doings forsooth!

COLL

Mak, is that the truth?
Now take out that southern tooth
    And stick in a flea!

GYB

The devil in your eye, to a blow I'll fain treat you.

DAW

Mak, do ye know me not? By God, I could beat you.

MAK

(throwing back his cloak). God keep you, all three, Now I wil
greet you. You are a fair company!

COLL

Ah, now he remembers, the cheat!

QYB

Thou shrew, jokes are cheap.
When so late a man goes
What else can folk suppose?
You've a bad name, God knows,
For stealing sheep!

MAK

True as steel am I, all men know and say.
But I have a sickness grips me night and day;
My belly is hungry, it is out of play!

DAW

Seldom does the devil die by the way!

MAK

Therefore Full sore am I, and ill,
Though I stand stone still,
I've not et my fill
This month and more.

COLL

How fares thy wife, by my hood, how, ask I?

MAK

She lies down, by the Rood, at the fire close by
And a houseful of home brew she drinks nigh.
I'll speed any good thing she may try
    Else to do!

MAK

She eats as fast as may be,
And every year there'll a day be
She brings forth another baby,
    And sometimes two,

Were I more kind, and richer in purse,
She'd still eat me out of house and home, sirs.
She's a foul-favored wench, if ye look close, by God's curse.
No one knows, or hears, I trow, of a worse,
    Not any!
I would fain proffer
To give all in my coffer
Tomorrow, to offer
    Her burying-penny!

GYB

Faith, so weary and worn is none in this shire.
I must sleep, though I be shorn of part of my hire.
(Lies down.)

DAW

I'm half naked, forlorn, and would fain have a fire.

COLL

I'm weary; since morn I've run in the mire
    Keep watch, do!
(Lies down also.)

GYB

Nay, I'll lie down hereby And to sleep I'll try.

DAW

As good a man's son am I
    As any of you.
(He lies down with the rest.)

MAK

I'll hinder you from talking at your ease,
    Indeed.
(Lies down between them.)
From my top to my toe
Manus tuas commendo
Pontio Pilato.
    Christ's cross me speed. *(Turns and sleeps.)*
(All are snoring loudly. MAK wakes and rises stealthily.)

MAK

Now 'twere time for a man that lacks what he would

To creep secretly into a fold
And nimbly to work, and not too bold
For he might fear discovery, if it were told
 At the ending.
Now were time for to revel
But he needs good counsel And
fain would he fare well
 And has but little for spending.
(He draws a circle around the sleepers.)

Draw about you a circle round as the moon,
And now I have done it, till it be noon
Ye shall lie stone still, until I have done
And I shall stay there till I've had my fun.
 On hight *(Lifts hand.)*
Over your heads my hand I lift.

Out go your eyes!   Gone is your sight!
But yet I must make better shift
    And it be right.
Lord, what a hard sleep may ye all have here!
I was never a shepherd, but I'll learn, that's clear!
If the flock be scared, I shall nip it here!
(Swings his cloak.)
    How, one draws hitherward, now mends our cheer
    From sorrow.
(He peers out.)
A fat sheep, I dare say,
A good fleece, I dare lay.
My friends, while I may,
    This sheep will I borrow!
(Exit, chasing after sheep.)

SCENE II. MAK's *ramshackle hut.*
(Enter MAK *with sheep under cloak, knocks on door of hut.)*

MAK

How, Gill, art thou in?   Get us some light!

GILL *(within).*

Who makes such a din this time of the night?
I am set for to spin, I think not I might
Rise, for a penny to win, I curse them on hight.
    So fares
A housewife that has been
Always pestered between
    For such small chores.

MAK

Goodwife, open the latch, see'st not what I bring?

GILL

I'll draw the latch bolt.   Come in, my sweeting.
(She opens.)

MAK

Yea, though think not how long thou keep me standing.
(She sees the s'heep.)

GILL

By the naked neck thou'rt like for to hang!

MAK

Go way!
I am worthy my meat,
For in a trice I can get
More than they who strive and sweat
    All the day long.
Thus it fell to my lot, Gill, I had such grace!

GILL
It were a foul blot to be hanged for this case.

MAK

I've escaped it oft, in many a place.

GILL

But so long goes pot to water, man says,
   At last Comes it home broken.

MAK

Well I know the token.
But let it never be spoken!
   Come, help me fast!
I would he were flayed, I'd gladly eat.
This twelvemonth I long for good sheep meat.

GILL

If they come in here again and hear the sheep bleat—

MAK

I'll be caught again, that were a cold sweat.
   Go bar
   The gate door.

GILL

Yes, Mak, for if they come at thy back-

MAK

Then would I fare, by all the pack
Devilish sore. (GILL *goes to cradle.*)

GILL

A good place I have spied, since thou can'st none.
Here shall he abide, till they be gone.
In my cradle he'll hide. Let me alone,
And I shall lie beside in childbed and groan.

MAK

To bed!
And I shall say thou gavest light
To a man-child this night.

GILL

Now well is me, day bright
That ever I was bred.
This is a good trick and a far cast,
Yet a woman's advice helps at the last.
Look sharp no one spies. Go thou back, fast!

MAK

I'll come, ere they rise, if blows no cold blast.
I'll go sleep.

Still sleepeth all this company
And I shall creep there privately
As if it never had been me
    That stole their sheep.   *(ᴱˣˡᵗ* MAK

SCENE III. *The Field again.*   *The stars are shining.*

COLL

Resurrex a mortuis! (Sits up.) Reach me a hand.
Judas carnas Dominus! I can scarce stand
My foot's asleep, my mouth dry as sand.
I thought we laid us down in England!
Yea, verily!

                 GYB (sitting up).

Lord, I have slept well.
As lively as an eel,
So light do I feel
    As leaf on a tree!

                 DAW (rising}.

Benidicite be herein. My body is shaking
My heart is cut out of my skin with its making.
Who shouts all this din? Sets my head to aching.
I'll do him in! Hark, fellows, be waking!
    Four of us were here.
See ye aught of Mak now?
We were waking ere thou.

GYB

I'll make it my vow
Not once did he stir.

DAW

Methought he was lapped in a wolf's skin!
So are many, these days, but the wolf is within!
Methought, while we napped, he came with a 'gin
And a fat sheep trapped, making no din.

GYB

Be still.
Thy dream makes thee mad.
It's a nightmare thou had
God bring good out of bad
If it be his will.
Rise, Mak, for shame, too long dost thou lie!

MAK

Now Christ's holy name be with us for aye!
What's this, by Saint James, I can't move if I try!
My body's the same, my neck's all awry.
  Enough, perdie!
(They help him up.)
Many thanks. Since yestreen
Now by Saint Steven
I was plagued by a dream
  Knocked the heart out of me.

I thought my Gill croaked and travailed full sad Till the crack of
dawn, to bear me a lad. To add to our flock. Of that I'm not glad,
I have more to care for than ever I had.
  Oh, my head!
A house full of young bairns,
(The devil knock out their brains.)
Woe is him who many children gains,
  And thereto no bread!
Ill come, by your leave, to Gill as I thought.
Come, look in my sleeve, be sure I steal naught
I am loath you to grieve, or from ye take aught.

DAW

I'll may'st thou thrive. Go!!
(To others). Would we had sought
  This mom
If all our flock were there
I'll go count them before.
Let us meet.

GYB

Where, for sure?

DAW

At the crooked thorn.
(They go out in different directions,)

SCENE IV. MAK's *Hut again,*   *(Enter M*AK

MAK *(hammering on the door),*

Open up!   Look who's here.   How long must I stand?

GILL

Who's making such gear.   Who walks in the land?

MAK

Ha, Gill, what cheer?   It is your husband.

GILL

Here comes the Devil and his band.
    Sir Guile! Lo, he shouts with a note
Like a pig stuck in the throat.
Not a minute can I devote
    To work any while.

MAK

What a pother she makes to be waked from her doze!
Only pleasure she takes, and curls up her toes.

GILL

Why? Who runs? Who wakes, who comes, who goes?
Who brews, who bakes, who croaks, who crows?
  And also
It is grief to behold
Now in hot, now in cold
Woeful is the household
  That no woman doth know.
  What luck hast thou had with the shepherds, Mak?

MAK

The last word they said when I turned my back Was, "go see if
we have all the sheep in the pack." They'll be mad, I wot, when
they see what they lack!
  Perdie!
But howso the game go
I'll be suspect, whether or no (poor fellow)
And they'll raise a great bellow
  And cry "Out" on me!

GILL

Thou must use thy sleight.
Yea, that's not ill
I'll swaddle him right in my cradle with skill.
Were a worse plight, I'd find a way still.
I'll lie down forthright. Tuck me in!
MAK

That I will.

GILL

And behind!
(He tucks her in behind.)

MAK

If Coll come, and his marrow
They'll nip us full narrow,
But I'll cry out "haro"
(See the Cry of Haro, time of William the Conqueror.)
    If the sheep they do find.

GILL

Hark, I hear them can, they'll be here anon.
Come, make ready all, and sing thou alone.
(MAK *sings a lullaby.*)
Sing lullaby loud, for now I must groan
And cry to the wall on Mary and John
    Full sore.

Sing lullaby fast
When thou hear them at last
If I play not a shrewd cast
    Never trust me more.

SCENE V. *On The Moor*

(This scene may be cut,)

DAW

Ah, Coll, good morn, why sleepest thou not?

COLL

Alack that I was ever born, we have a foul blot!
A fat sheep have we lost.

DAW

God forbid! Say it not!

GYB

Who would do us that scorn, it were a foul spot!

COLL

Some shrew!
I have searched, with my dogs
All Horbury bogs
And of fifteen hogs
    Found all but one ewe.

DAW

Trust me, if you will, by St. Thomas of Kent.
Either Mak or wife Gill their way there bent.

COLL

Peace, man, be still. I saw where he went.
Thou dost slander him ill, and should repent
Indeed!

GYB

So may I thrive, Perdie
Let me die where I be
I still say it was he
    Did that deed.

DAW

Go we thither, speed. Run fast on our feet.
I shall never eat bread till I know it complete.

COLL

No more meat or drink till I him meet.

GYB

In no place will I bed till I him greet.
    My brother!
One vow will I plight,
Till I have him in sight
I'll not sleep one night
    Where I sleep another! *(They go out.)*

SCENE VI.   MAK's *Hovel*
("MAK *and* GILL *are making a terrible din, alternately groaning and singing.)*

DAW

Hark, what a row they make. List to Mak how he croon!

COLL

Never heard I voice break so clear out of tune.
Call him!

GYB

Mak, there, wake up, undo the door soon.

MAK *(within)*.

Who's that cries out as if it were noon
    Aloft? Who's there, I say?

DAW

Good Mak, if 'twere day-

MAK

As far as ye may,
    Pray ye, speak soft!
    My poor sick wife in such grievous throes
    I were liefer dead than she suffer such woes.
    (He opens and they come in.)
GILL

(Waving a weak hand from the bed).
Go your way, well sped.
(They come in nearer.)
          Oh, now my pain grows.
Each footstep ye tread goes right through my nose.
So loud, woe's me!

COLL

Tell us, Mak, if ye may
How fare ye, I say?

MAK (angrily).

Are ye still here, today?
    Now, how fare ye?
Ye have run in the mire and are wet still, a bit.
I'll make ye a fire, if ye fain would sit.
A nurse would I hire, can ye help me a bit?
Well quit is my hire, my dream had truth in it.
    This season
I have children, ye know
Plenty more than will do.
But we drink as we brew.
    That is but reason.
    I would ye would eat, ere ye go. Methinks that ye sweat.

GYB

Nay, our mood mends not with drink or meat.

MAK

Why, Sir, what ails ye but good?   (Ails ye aught but good?)

DAW

    Yea, our sheep on their feet
Are stole as they go. Our loss it is great.

MAK

Good sirs, drink!

Had I been there
The thief had bought it full sore.

COLL

Marry, some think ye it were
And that I also think.

GYB

Mak, some men think it should be ye.
DAW

Either ye, or your spouse, so say we.

MAK

Now, if you make suspect either Gill or me,
Come and search our house, then may ye see
    Who stole her
    If ye see any sheep's foot
    Either goat, cow or stoat—
For Gill, my wife, rose not.
    Long since she laid here.

As I am true and honest, to God I shall pray
This be the first meal I shall eat this day.

COLL

Mak, as I have weal, I advise thee, I say
"He learned quickly to steal that could not say nay!"

GILL *(screaming)*.

Go, my death you've dealt!
Out, ye thieves, nor come again.
Ye come but to rob me, that's plain.

MAK

Hear ye not how she groans amain?
Your hearts should melt!

GILL

From my child begone! Go not near. There's the door!

MAK

If ye knew all she's borne, your hearts would be sore.
Ye do wrong, I warn, thus to come in before
A woman in childbirth. But I say no more.

GILL

Oh, my belly! I die!
I vow to God so mild
If ever I you beguiled
Then I will eat this child
That doth in cradle lie!

MAK *(hiding a smile)*

Peace, woman, in thy pain, and cry not so.
Thou dost hurt my brain, and fill me with woe.

COLL

I trow, our sheep is slain, what think ye two?
Our search is in vain, we may as well go.
For what matters?

I can find no flesh
Hard or nesh
Salt nor fresh
    Save two empty platters.

Of any sheep, tame or wild, that we see
None of our flock smells as loud as he.

GILL

May God joy and bliss in my child give me!

COLL (apologizing).

We have aimed amiss. Deceived were we.
    Surely, each one. Sir, our lady
him save, Is your child a knave?

MAK

Any lord might him have
    This child for a son.

GYB

Come, Mak, friends we'll be, for we are at one.

MAK

We? Count not on me. Amends I get none.
Farewell, all three, I'll be glad when you're gone!

DAW

Fair words there may be, but love ye have none
   This year.
(They go to the door and stand in it.)

                 COLL (at door).

Gave ye the child anything?

                 GYB

Nay, not one farthing.

DAW

Back again will I fling.
   Wait me here. Mak, take it not ill if I come to thy child.

MAK *(hastily).*

Nay, wake it not, though art too loud and wild.

DAW

Thy child I will not grieve If only by your
leave I come and to him give But sixpence.

MAK *(stepping between).*

Nay, go way, he sleeps.

DAW

Methinks'I hear he peeps.

MAK

When he wakens, he weeps. I pray, go hence!

DAW

Give me leave him to kiss, and lift up the clout.
(He lifts the covers.)
What the devil is this?   He has a long snout!

COLL (from door).

He be marked amiss, let be, come, we wait about.

DAW

Ill-spun the web,comes always foul out.
Just so! Ho! He is like to our sh'.-ep!

GYB

(Coming back and looking into cradle)
Now, Mak, may I peep?

COLL

I trow, kind will creep
Where it may not go!

GYB

This is a smart trick and a far cast.
It was a high fraud.

DAW

Yes, it was.
Take hold this woman and bind her fast.
Thou false scade, thou shalt hang at last.
So shalt thou!
Look you there, how they swaddle
His four feet in the middle.
Saw I never in cradle
A horned lad till now!

MAK

Leave be, have peace, leave her go, there!
I begat that child, and this woman him bare.

COLL

What Devil's name has he got, Mak? Look ye, Mak's heir!

GYB

Let be thy jest. Now God give him care,
    I say.

GILL

As pretty a child is he
    As sits on any woman's knee
A dillydown, perdee.
(She rocks the cradle.)
To make a man gay.

DAW

I know him by the ear mark, that's a good token.

MAK

I tell ye sirs, hark, his nose was broken.
A clerk told me it would be misspoken.
COLL

This is a false work. I would fain be wroken.
    Get weapon.

GILL *(in desperation).*

He was taken by an elf,
I saw it myself
When the clock struck twelf,
    He was misshapen!

GYB

Ye two are well mated, peas in a pod.

DAW

Since they uphold their theft, let's strike them dead.

MAK(whining).

If I have done ill, strike off my head
And do your will!

COLL

Sirs, for this deed, take my advice instead,
    For this trespass.
    We will neither curse nor fight
Nor dispute our right.
We'll tie him up tight
    And toss him in canvas.
(They toss him in a sheet.)

(If desired to cut this action, MAK *can run out the door and th*
others follow.)

SCENE VI. *On The Moor, Night.*

COLL

Lord, I am sore, about for to burst.
Faith, I can no more, therefore I will rest.

GYB

Like a sheep of seven-score he weighed in my fist.
To sleep an hour, I think that I list

DAW

Now I pray you
Lie down on this green.
(He spreads boughs.)

COLL

On these thieves, I will yet-

DAW

Why, what shall ye get?
Let be, I say you.

(The skies lighten suddenly and an angel appears, singing Gloria In Excels is.)

ANGEL

Rise, herdsmen, rise, for Christ is born
To rend the fiend that Adam had lorn
The Saviour of all, this night is he born.

His behests
To Bethlehem go see
Where lies this baby
In a crib full poorly
Betwixt two beasts.

(Sky fades out leaving a single star.)
ANGEL *disappears.)*

COLL

This was a stranger song than ever I heard.
It is a marvel thus to be scared.

GYB

Of God's son he spoke from heavenward
And on the hill all heaven's guard
Appeared.

DAW

He spoke of a barn In Bethlehem, I you warn,
There's a sign in yon star. Let us seek him there.

GYB

Heard you not, pray, what was that song?

DAW

Marry, three briefs to a long.
Full loud and clear, it had no crotchet wrong.

COLL

Sing, too, I can, for to sing us among.
　　Good men!

GYB

Let's see how ye croon.
Can ye bark at the moon?

DAW

Hold your tongue, have done.

COLL

Let's go, then.

GYB

To Bethlehem we should haste along,
I am afeared we tarry too long.

DAW

Be merry, not sad.   Of mirth is our song.
   Be everlasting glad, have a drink, it's no wrong.
   Make a noise.

Hie we thither right merry
If we be wet and weary
Still, we'll find the child and lady,
   We cannot lose.
(They sing an old carol.)

SCENE VII. *The Stable at Bethlehem,* MARY *and the child*
JESUS. *(This can be represented by a tableau behind gauze, o*
by shadows if desired; soft music of Adeste Fideles.)

COLL

Hail, comely and clean, hail, young child!
Hail, God, who made a maiden so mild.
Thou hast cowed at last the devil so wild
The false beguiler now goes beguiled.
   Look, he merries,
Lo, he laughs, my sweeting!
A welcome meeting,
I have brought this greeting,
   Have a bob of cherries!

GYB

Hail, sovereign saviour, for thou hast us sought!
Hail, noble child and flower of all things wrought,
Hail, full of favour, that made all*of nought!
Hail, I kneel and cower, look, a bird I have brought

To this barn far.
Hail, Hail, little tiny mop
Of our creed thou are the crop.
I would drink to thee in my cup.
Little day star!

DAW

Hail, darling dear, full of Godhead!
I pray thee be near when I have need
Hail, sweet is thy cheer, my heart would bleed
To see thee sit here in so poor a weed
    With no pennies.
Hail, put forth thy dall *(hand)*
I bring thee but a ball,
Have it, and play withal,
    And go to tennis.

MARY

The father of Heaven, God Omnipotent
That made all in heaven, his son has he sent.
My name he did name, and blest me ere he went,
And a child was conceived, full might, as he meant.
    And now he is born.
To keep you from woe
1 shall pray him so,
Tell it forth, as ye go,
    And mind on this morn!

COLL

Farewell, lady so fair to behold
With thy child on thy knee.

GYB

But he lies full cold.
Lord, well is me. Now we go, behold!

DAW

Forsooth, already it seems to be told
    Full oft!

COLL

What grace have we found!

GYB

Come forth, tell it around.

DAW

To sing are we bound.
    Let us sing aloft!

(They sing,)
        To Bethlehem, that noble place
        As by prophecy said it was . . . etc.

        Salvator Mundi Natus est!

        Be ye merry
        In this feast

        In quo Salvator natus est!

PRODUCTION NOTES

I have tried not to make too many cuts and changes in this very ancient English Play which has come down to us through hundreds of years with all its rich language of rhyme and alliteration. Care must be taken not to lose the music and pattern of the verses. The play itself is a fusion of the rough peasant humor of the period, and simple religious faith, and should be handled so as not to lose either quality. Although originally performed by human actors, the play can be done with hand puppets and perhaps even with marionettes. Some fine scenic effects are possible here - the snow falling, the stars coming out, the angel, or several angels, behind a gauze or translucent backdrop. A cut-out of the village of Bethlehem behind gauze, in the early scenes, and a Nativity tableau at the end, will be very effective. Christmas music on records or tape recorder can be faded in and out between scenes. This can be a very beautiful production if the director can manage to hold the mood and fuse the humor with the poetry in a delicate balance.

Made in the USA
Monee, IL
09 January 2021